MARRIAGE IS FOREVER
...some days longer

Gene Perret

COVER ILLUSTRATION
David Webber Merrell

INSIDE ILLUSTRATIONS
Vicky Snow

WitWorks™

2039 West Lewis Avenue, Phoenix, Arizona 85009
Telephone: (602) 712-2200
Web site: www.witworksbooks.com

Publisher — Win Holden
Managing Editor — Bob Albano
Associate Editor — Evelyn Howell
Associate Editor — PK Perkin McMahon
Art Director — Mary Winkelman Velgos
Director of Photography — Peter Ensenberger
Production Director — Cindy Mackey
Production Coordinator — Kim Ensenberger

Library of Congress Catalog Number: 2002104113
ISBN 1-893860-68-X

FIRST EDITION, published in 2002.
Printed in the United States.

Book designer — Mary Winkelman Velgos

LIKE GOOD WINE,

MARRIAGE GETS BETTER

WITH AGE . . . ONCE

YOU LEARN TO KEEP

A CORK IN IT.

I've enjoyed all these years married to the same woman.

Of course, after all these years married to me, she's not quite the same woman.

NEVER HOLD A GRUDGE IN A MARRIAGE.

Get your revenge early and get it out of the way.

Marriage begins

with a three-word phrase . . .

"I love you."

But it endures

with a two-word phrase . . .

"Yes, Dear."

We've had some good times together, and we've had some bad times together.

AND TOGETHER WE'VE DECIDED THAT MOST OF THE BAD TIMES WERE MY FAULT.

To me, you're my

reason for living.

To you, I'm your reason

for buying a Dustbuster.

Since our marriage,
there have been
a lot of good times.

**I'VE EVEN BEEN INVITED
TO A FEW OF THEM.**

If I had listened to

my mother I would

have been a doctor.

And if you had listened to your mother,
I would have been a patient.

I ALWAYS THOUGHT YOU WERE

too good for me.

EVERYONE IN YOUR FAMILY,

EXCEPT YOU,

AGREED WITH ME.

On our wedding day

your mother said to me,

*"I wish you were
my own son."*

"That way it would be

illegal for you

to marry my daughter."

LIFE IS SHORT . . .

BUT MARRIAGE

CAN MAKE IT

SEEM LONGER.

YOU'VE ALWAYS HAD A GREAT

SENSE OF HUMOR.

I remember when you announced that

you were marrying me, all your

friends said, "You're joking."

Our marriage

has always been

a 50-50 proposition . . .

with the possible

exception

of closet space.

Does this say something
about marriage?

**YOU STILL HAVE THE
DRESS YOU WERE MARRIED IN.
MY TUX HAD TO BE
BACK IN THE SHOP BY MONDAY.**

Sure, we've had

a few disagreements

over the years,

but they were all quickly

forgotten . . .

once I accepted the blame.

EVEN THOUGH OURS WAS

love at first sight,

I REMEMBER YOUR FAMILY SAYING,

"PLEASE . . . GO BACK AND

TAKE A SECOND LOOK."

I swore when we married

that you were too good for me,

but now after all these years

we get along beautifully.

Did I go up to your
level, or did you
come down to mine?

We've had a few of our

dreams
come true

since our wedding day.

Of course, when you sleep as much as we do, some of the dreams HAVE to come true.

**WE'VE HAD
GOOD TIMES,
AND WE'VE HAD
BAD TIMES.**

What we haven't
had is much
SPARE TIME.

We have no "boss"
in our marriage.

*That's because
neither one of us
wants the job.*

I learned early
that marriage is a
give and take
proposition.

**WHAT I DON'T GIVE,
YOU TAKE ANYWAY.**

**WE'VE
GROWN OLD
GRACEFULLY
TOGETHER.**

*Who knows?
Apart we might have
stayed young.*

To make a marriage last,

try to say

"I love you"

at least as many times

as you say,

"What's for dinner?"

**WE VOWED EARLY IN OUR MARRIAGE
NEVER TO GO TO BED ANGRY.**

The dog loves it

because many nights

she has the Beautyrest

entirely to herself.

To this day

I'll never know

what you saw in me.

But whatever you saw,
I hope it's still in there.

My love has grown

over the years

. . . as have many other
parts of me.

TAKING YOU AS MY BRIDE WAS

THE MOST EXCITING MOMENT

OF MY LIFE . . . IN THE

NON-SPORTING EVENT

CATEGORY.

We've had both good

and bad times together . . .

often while attending

the same movie.

WE WERE

young and foolish

WHEN WE GOT MARRIED.

Unfortunately, we've outgrown the

YOUNG part.

It's been fun
raising our children
and watching
them grow.

I handled the watching part.

**WE HAVE A
PERFECT RECORD.**

In all these years
I've never forgotten
our anniversary, and
you've never forgotten
to remind me
it was coming.

MY JOB WAS TO MAKE ALL THE BIG
DECISIONS IN THIS MARRIAGE.

MY FIRST DECISION
WAS TO LET YOU MAKE
ALL THE REMAINING DECISIONS.

I had
the whole world
at my feet
when we were
first married.

Now I have trouble finding
my shoes in the morning.

Everyone is looking for the PERFECT mate.

It's a good starting point from which to start making much needed improvements.

Through our years together you've

learned to accept my weaknesses.

YOU RARELY ASK ME TO DO
ANYTHING THAT REQUIRES EITHER
COORDINATION OR INTELLIGENCE.

Our marriage was

made in heaven,

but they sent the bill

to your parents.

**OUR WEDDING
WAS MANY YEARS AGO.**

The celebration
continues to this day.

Marriage

IS NATURE'S WAY OF SAYING,

"YOU DON'T NEED

THAT MUCH OF THE COVERS

ANYWAY."

We can get
through anything
together.

In fact, we already may have.

LIFE WITH YOU IS ONE ADVENTURE AFTER ANOTHER.

Isn't that the same thing that Robin Hood said to his Merry Men?

YOU'VE MADE ME

WHAT I AM

TODAY.

(Someone has to take the blame.)

Teamwork
**is what makes
our marriage
successful.**

**OF COURSE, IT'S ALSO WHAT MADE
STARS OF THE THREE STOOGES.**

WE'VE BEEN

TOGETHER THROUGH

THICK AND THIN . . .

BUT ENOUGH ABOUT

MY GRAVIES.

**ON THE AVERAGE,
YOUR PARENTS LIKED ME.**

Your mother knew
you could have done better;

your father thought
you could have done worse.

From time to time

I like to look at

our wedding

album

and relive my old waistline.

Our love
has grown as
my hairline
has receded.

You've
made a new man
out of me.

You must have; the old one
used to fit into my suits.

Together

we've discovered

that two can live

as cheaply

as one . . . but

only for about

half as long.

The preacher said,

"Do you take this man for better or for worse?"

?
♥

And you asked if
he could be more specific.

**I once swore
I would do anything for you.**

*Of course, at the time
I didn't realize that you
would draw up
a new list every week.*

You're not only my spouse,

you're also my best friend.

As one or the other

could you lend me 20 bucks

till payday?

. . . How about 15 bucks from each of you?

Before we were married

I promised you

the world on a string.

**BUT REMEMBER,
STRING WAS MUCH CHEAPER THEN.**

OUR MARRIAGE

HAS WORKED BECAUSE I'VE

ALWAYS FELT FREE

TO DO WHATEVER

I WANTED.

**AND YOU'VE ALWAYS FELT FREE
TO TELL ME WHAT IT WAS I WANTED.**

WE'VE BEEN MARRIED

so long

THAT SOME OF THE TIES

I WORE WHEN WE

WERE COURTING

HAVE COME BACK

INTO STYLE . . .

THREE OR FOUR TIMES.

Many of our friends

are no longer married

to each other,

and some who

are still married

to each other

are no longer friends.

WE'VE HAD
A LOT OF LAUGHS
THROUGH THE YEARS.

SOMETIMES
AT EACH OTHER.

I'm glad

you married me

when you did.

*My gain was
"Mr. Right's" loss.*

WE'VE HAD A FEW DISAGREEMENTS OVER THE YEARS, BUT WE'VE ALWAYS WORKED THEM OUT.

I'm always willing to take the blame
for being right.

Our marriage is a compromise.

**I'm willing to forgive you
when you're less than perfect, and
you're willing to forgive me
for not being Elvis Presley.**

Over the years
our love has matured,
and so have you.

**I PROMISE I'LL GROW UP
EVENTUALLY.**

I ALWAYS

THOUGHT

YOU WERE

TOO GOOD

FOR ME.

You're finally coming around to my way of thinking.

**SOME OF THE DREAMS
WE HAD TOGETHER
HAVE NOT COME TRUE.**

But then again,
some of those that have come true
are not paid for yet.

There have been times

in our marriage when

even I thought

your mother might

have been right

about me.

YOU'VE MADE ME

A BETTER PERSON — BUT

YOU'VE STILL GOT

A LOT OF WORK TO DO.

WE'LL ALWAYS HAVE

LAUGHTER IN OUR MARRIAGE . . .

AS LONG AS WE HAVE

our wedding

album.

You've
made me what
I am today. . .

about 15 pounds
overweight.

You're the one who remains

cool and calm in every emergency.

I'M THE ONE
WHO USUALLY PROVIDES
THE EMERGENCIES.

We've kept a
sense of humor in our
marriage.

**THAT'S BECAUSE EVERY
TIME YOUR FAMILY LOOKS
AT ME THEY LAUGH.**

AFTER ALL THESE

YEARS OF MARRIAGE,

YOU'RE STILL

THE PERSON

I WANT TO

GO THROUGH LIFE

LOSING ARGUMENTS TO.

THROUGH THE YEARS
MY LOVE FOR YOU
HAS GROWN.

BUT MY AVAILABLE
CLOSET SPACE
HAS DWINDLED.

You've

turned me into

a new man.

**The old one you've probably
made into a planter.**

I would give up almost
everything for you.

In fact, I think I might

have to because

I'm running out of

closet space for my stuff.

You and I both agree

that one person

in this marriage is perfect.

We often disagree, though, on who that is.

In our marriage,

I may not always be

right, but I'll defend

to the death

my right to pretend

that I am.

*Our love has
grown
over the years.*

SOMETHING has . . . none
of my trousers fit anymore.

WE'VE ALWAYS

COMPROMISED

IN OUR MARRIAGE.

**Sometimes
we do things your way;
other times
we don't do them mine.**

WE'VE BEEN MARRIED

SO LONG

WE'RE LIKE TWO PEOPLE

joined together

AT THE CHECKBOOK.

I'M YOUR PARTNER

FOR LIFE — EVEN

ON THOSE DAYS

WHEN I SEEM

LIFELESS.

We promised

never to go to bed

angry with each other.

**Some days that really
eats into my naptime.**

When we were married,

some of our friends

gave us a year.

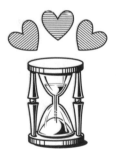

Fortunately, we got
time added on for good behavior.

IN MARRIAGE

I'VE FOUND THAT

TWO CAN LIVE AS CHEAPLY

AS ONE . . . UNLESS

ONE OF THEM

HAS A CREDIT CARD.

In all our

years of marriage

you've never tried

to change me into

a better person.

And you'll probably agree

that neither have I.

Sure I've got my faults, but

look on the bright side . . .

They give you something

to talk to your mother about

on the phone.

I've often said

I'm nobody's fool,

but you correct me

and say

I'm your fool.

You and I go together

like two peas in a pod . . .

Only my part of the pod

has less closet space.

OUR LOVE

HAS STAYED

FOREVER YOUNG.

Don't you wish we had?

Love makes the world go 'round.

**Sometimes it keeps me
spinning pretty well, too.**

You married me
for better or worse.

**I think I've delivered
in both of those areas.**

We've navigated

the sea of matrimony

quite well together

for many years now.

Although, I do feel I've been doing most of the rowing.

EVERY

MARRIAGE

HAS

PROBLEMS.

In your case,

you married one.

Before we were married

I felt you were too good for me.

YOU DISAGREED.

Thank goodness, that was

the first of many arguments

I've lost.

You married me

for better or worse,

richer or poorer,

in sickness or in health.

Judging from the way my clothes fit,
BIGGER AND HEAVIER
should have been in there, too.

YOU LOOKED BEAUTIFUL
AS MY BRIDE, AND
YOU LOOK BEAUTIFUL
TODAY.

I LOOKED HANDSOME
AS A GROOM, AND
ONE OUT OF TWO
IS NOT BAD.

Some said we were

young and foolish

when we were wed.

WE SHOWED THEM.

Now we're

old and foolish.

Some people call you

MY BETTER HALF

*Their intentions are good, but their math
is woefully underestimated.*

"They lived happily ever after"

is not only a good ending

to a fairy tale,

it's also the only

prenuptial agreement

we've ever had.

If I had it to do all over,

I'd marry you again

. . . provided Meg Ryan

was still unavailable.

**WE WERE
MADE FOR
EACH OTHER.**

You're a great cook,
and I'm a great eater.

SOMEDAY

I HOPE TO BE

AS SUCCESSFUL AS

ALL THOSE GUYS

YOU TELL ME

YOU COULD HAVE

MARRIED.

All of our years

of marriage

and raising a family

was only practice

so we'd be good enough

to baby-sit

our grandchildren.

Periodically

you give your old clothes

away to the needy.

**I give mine away to people
who apparently have more
closet space than I have.**

Years ago
you wanted
children
so badly

you married one.

I'll be the first
to say that
I haven't always been
the perfect spouse.

**WELL, I GUESS I'LL BE
THE SECOND TO SAY IT.**

It took you a long time to

bring me home

to meet your parents.

THAT WAS PARTLY THEIR FAULT.

EVERY TIME THEY HEARD

I WAS COMING, THEY MOVED.

When we were
young lovers
you used to run
your slender fingers
through my hair.

We're still lovers,
your fingers are still slender,
but we have no idea
where the hair has gone.

A good husband is like
an airplane landing.

**IT DOESN'T
HAVE TO BE PERFECT,
SO LONG AS
YOU CAN CONTROL IT.**

We've been married
so long we're
starting to think alike.

For instance, even
when we disagree now,
we both think I'm wrong.

When you introduced

me to your folks,

your Dad said,

"You could have

done worse."

Your Mom said,

"How?"

Our marriage
is a true partnership.

Apparently, I'm the silent partner.

I WEAR

THE PANTS

IN THE

FAMILY.

**That's because there's no room left in my
part of the closet to hang them up.**

It seems like overnight

all of our wonderful

wedding gifts

have turned into

valuable antiques.

I'd love to

marry you

all over again.

We could use some new china.

Once I promised
you the world
with a picket fence
around it.

**THEN IT DAWNED ON ME THAT
I'D HAVE TO PAINT THAT FENCE.**

Love, they say,
makes the world
go 'round.

Thankfully, we're still spinning,
but at a sensible speed.

I love you more today

than yesterday,

but not as much

as tomorrow.

*Which, if my math
is correct, gives me
tonight off.*

YOU'VE ALWAYS

BEEN THERE FOR ME

WHENEVER

I NEEDED YOU — WHICH

IS PRETTY MUCH

ALL THE TIME

... EXCEPT WHEN

I'M WATCHING FOOTBALL.

I've learned

in marriage

that a woman's work

is never done.

And even when it is,

she has to get busy

trying to get the man

to do his work.

I ALWAYS KNEW
WE WOULD
GROW OLD TOGETHER.

**I JUST DIDN'T EXPECT YOU
TO GIVE ME SO MUCH
OF A HEAD START.**

We've always shared the load.

**You do your share;
I'm the load.**

OVER THE YEARS,

your love has kept me young.

NOW IF I COULD JUST FIND SOMETHING TO KEEP MY WEIGHT DOWN.

Think what would

have happened

if we had never

been introduced.

**You would have spent all these years
married to a perfect stranger.**

YOU'VE
MADE ME
WHAT I AM
TODAY.

You'll have to decide whether that's a compliment or a complaint.

I took you out for a

romantic dinner

the night I proposed to you.

**I remember you were so surprised,
you almost dropped your tray.**

ANYTHING YOU ASK
I WOULD DO GLADLY
FOR YOU.

Just add it to the list of things
you've already asked me to do
but I haven't gotten around to yet.

I have no secrets

from you . . .

and even if I did,

I wouldn't tell you

about them.

If I had to,

I'd marry you

all over again.

**I'd just need a
larger size tux this time.**

Our love has mellowed
over the years.

Mellowed — that's

a nice word meaning

"I'm getting too old for

this kind of stuff."

**I KNOW YOU'LL
ALWAYS BE THERE
WHENEVER I NEED YOU.**

*And you know that
whenever you're there,
I'll probably find a reason
to need you.*

We've had a few
disagreements
over the years,
but they're all
forgotten now.

Do you disagree with that?

*Sure, we've had
some harsh words
in our marriage.*

**In fact, you've had a few
that I'd never heard before.**

My wedding band is precious to me.

IT'S ONE OF THE FEW THINGS WE OWN THAT'S PAID FOR.

If I remember correctly,
it was you
who pursued me.

*And you wouldn't give up
until I finally caught you.*

When we were

young and in love

we had that

"we can do anything"

bravado.

We still have that

"we can do anything" bravado,

but now it's tempered with a touch of

"but let's not hurt ourselves

in the process."

Two can live

as cheaply as one . . .

if one doesn't

eat anything

or wear any clothes.

MARRIAGE

IS AN

INSTITUTION.

You have to be committed to it.

We don't agree on

everything, but

we do agree that

we both have

good taste

in spouses.

We've been together a long time.

We're either doing something right,
or neither one of us
is sharp enough to know that
we're doing something wrong.

THE TWO OF US
HAVE BECOME ONE.

We must have because my clothes
are getting so tight now it feels like
someone's in there with me.

**AFTER ALL THESE YEARS,
I'D MARRY YOU ALL OVER AGAIN.**

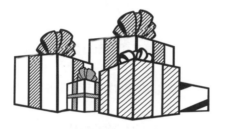

*A few of our friends
are rich enough now
to buy us better
wedding gifts.*

Of all the

smart things

I've done in my life,

marrying you is

number one.

So far I haven't done anything
else smart enough to qualify as
number two.

You've made me what I am today.

Now let's hear your side of the story.

WE HAVE THE

GREATEST

PRE-NUPTIAL

AGREEMENT

IN THE WORLD.

It's called "Love."